Brisbane
Travel Guide

Quick Trips Series

Table of Contents

Brisbane & Gold Coast

The sunshine state of Queensland, located in the northeast of Australia is one of the country's best tourist destinations. Queensland's largest city is the state capital of Brisbane and together with the neighbouring Gold Coast and Sunshine Coast has beautiful beaches, constant sunshine and some of the world's best watersports and activities.

Brisbane, with its youthful vibrancy has grown into a world city and is the fastest growing city in Australia. Located along the Brisbane River, from which it gets its name, this hilly city is a melting pot of nature and fast paced urban life. Truly a Commonwealth city by heart – many of the streets are named after the Royal family – it retains a unique heritage charm by preserving many of the historic buildings of the 19th century.

Brisbane is divided into a number of districts each an attraction in itself with unique sights. The Central Business District (CBD) is the "mini-Manhattan" of Brisbane with its multitude of skyscrapers. Located in the CBD is the Roma Street Parkland – the world's largest urban subtropical garden. The Inner North district with Fortitude Valley is the part of town that does not sleep, with its myriad of restaurants and nightclubs. Inner South is the only part of town that has a beach – the only one in the country in the middle of a city! The Inner West and East districts are the hilly regions with trendy restaurants and some stunning viewpoints. The West End is the haven for shopaholics – from the chic urban to the quirky alternative. The Bayside and Outer Suburbs are the residential quarters.

Located between Brisbane and the border of New South Wales is the coastal resort of Gold Coast with some of the most popular tourist spots on the east coast. Regarded as a part of Greater Brisbane, Gold Coast is conveniently connected by road and rail from the city and is regularly commuted by many locals for work or pleasure. Surfer's Paradise, the 'capital' of Gold Coast attracts a young crowd from not only different parts of the Australian east coast, but also from neighbouring New Zealand. With innumerable opportunities for world-class surfing and plenty of bars and nightclubs dotting the area, Gold Coast is aptly called the 'pilgrimage' for the youngsters.

BRISBANE, GOLD COAST & SUNSHINE COAST TRAVEL GUIDE

Located to the north of Brisbane is the Sunshine Coast with its collection of small towns, beaches, and hinterlands. In what is a complete contrast from its southern neighbours, the Sunshine Coast attracts the visitors with its natural beauty and relaxed ambience. With many beaches, a zoo, a national park, a state forest, and multitude of hiking and walking trails on the hills, it is the perfect getaway for the whole family.

Brisbane, Gold Coast, and the Sunshine Coast encapsulate many different tourist worlds into one – from the quiet hiking trails on the hills to the trendy restaurants on Mt Coot-tha, or from the beach parties on the Gold Coast to the relaxed afternoon in the Sunshine Coast beaches. From a quiet family outing to wild celebrations with friends, there is something on the plate for everyone.

🌐 Customs & Culture

Perfectly keeping in line with the vibrancy, Brisbane, Gold Coast and the Sunshine Coast have a lot to offer in music, arts, and culture. Brisbane is one of the major hotspots of music in the southern hemisphere. From the riverside to the historic theatres, there are a number of venues in the city where one can catch a music show or concert. South Bank is one of the major hubs in the city for music and is a must visit for any theatre or music lover. It is home to the Queensland Performing Arts Centre consisting of the Cremorne Theatre, Playhouse Theatre, Lyric Theatre, and Concert Hall. One can catch a performance of the Queensland Ballet, Queensland

Symphony Orchestra, or even a performance by one of the numerous choirs that perform in these venues regularly. The city also has a number of annual rock festivals including the Soundwave and Future Music Festival. The QUT Theatre Republic, Judith Wright Centre, and Metro Arts along with the South Bank region host a number of visual arts exhibitions all round the year.

Other then the classical Northern Rivers Symphony Orchestra and Operators Please, Gold Coast hosts a number of popular annual pop and rock festivals including the Big Day Out, V Festival, and Parklife.

The annual Royal Queensland Show (Ekka) and the Brisbane Festival are two of the biggest festivals in the Brisbane culture calendar. Held in the months of August and September, the festivals are held at various venues and features concerts, plays, exhibitions, circus, conferences, and family games. The festivals draw crowds not only from the suburbs but also from the neighboring cities. The 2-day Greek food festival of Paniyiri in May and the St George's International Film Festival in November are two other major events in the city calendar.

🌏 Geography

Brisbane, Gold Coast and the Sunshine Coast are located on the central east coast of Australia, about 730 km north of the closest major city – Sydney. Although this is one of the easternmost tourist destinations in the world and located deep down in the southern hemisphere, the popularity and attraction of the region means it is very well connected with the rest of the world.

The Brisbane Airport (IATA: BNE) - http://www.bne.com.au is located about 20 km north east of the city centre and connects Brisbane to not only other Australian cities and towns but to many major Asian, European, and American cities. It is to be noted that although the airport has separate domestic and international terminals about 3 km apart, both the terminals are used for domestic and international flights. One should verify the terminal beforehand to avoid delays. The terminals are connected by the AirTrain - http://www.airtrain.com.au/ and TBus - http://www.bne.com.au/parking-transport/transport-options. Both these services are available from early morning until 11:00 pm.

The BNE Airport is connected to the city through multiple road and rail options. The quickest is by AirTrain. The 30 minute ride costs $16 (Australian dollars) and connects to South Bank, Central, and Roma Street stations. Shuttle vans run by CoachTrans - http://www.con-x-ion.com/ cost about $20 for the journey which can take up to 1 hour to the city. Although one gets the facility of the hotel drop, the wait at the airport – because of the queue – could itself be over an hour. For quicker boarding one can buy a non-refundable ticket online. Taxis are readily available near the terminals and cost approximately $35 for the one way ride. This, of course, becomes a cheaper option than the shuttle if there are 2 or 3 passengers. Major rental

BRISBANE, GOLD COAST & SUNSHINE COAST TRAVEL GUIDE

cars like Avis and Hertz are also present at the airport for those who want to drive.

Brisbane has rail connections with Sydney, Canberra, and Melbourne through the Countrylink - http://www.nswtrainlink.info/. For those planning to be connected by rail with the suburbs and other parts of Queensland can opt for the Queensland Rail - http://www.queenslandrail.com.au.

Bus services from neighbouring cities are available from Greyhound Australia - http://www.greyhound.com.au/ and Premiere Transport Group - www.premierms.com.au. A return ticket from Melbourne to Brisbane (approx 17 hrs) costs around $90 if bought in advance online. Greyhound also offers hop-in-hop-off passes.

BRISBANE, GOLD COAST & SUNSHINE COAST TRAVEL GUIDE

Brisbane is connected by road through a number of Motorways and Highways including the A1, A2, A15, M1, and M2. For those planning to drive, it has to be kept in mind that Australia has a left-lane driving rule. Speed limits are 110 km per hr for highways and 50 km per hr for built-up areas. Speed limits are strictly enforced and driving even 5 km above the speed limit will incur a fine. To drive in Australia, one must be 21 years of age and have an International Driver's License in English.

For those planning to take the sea route, the Brisbane Terminal Cruise offers luxury cruises from Portside Wharf to neigbouring Australian cities. Located only 7 km from the airport, Portside Wharf is easily accessible from the Brisbane city centre, Gold Coast, and Sunshine Coast.

BRISBANE, GOLD COAST & SUNSHINE COAST TRAVEL GUIDE

Once in Brisbane, one can use the public transport operated by Translink - http://translink.com.au/. Public transport ticket in Brisbane is the most expensive in Australia costing $4 for a trip. An option is to buy the GoCard - http://translink.com.au/tickets-and-fares/go-card that provides a minimal discount. Ferries run by CityCats and CityFerries is a quick and unique way to commute within the city limits. Brisbane also has facilities for bicycles, especially for tourists with daily and weekly packages - http://www.citycycle.com.au/. Those visiting CBD, South Bank and other major tourist spots in the city can try the unique Green Cabs - http://www.greencabs.net.au/ - a carbon free rickshaw ride in the city limits.

BRISBANE, GOLD COAST & SUNSHINE COAST TRAVEL GUIDE

Gold Coast, at a distance of only 70 km from Brisbane, is directly served by the Gold Coast Airport (IATA: OOL) - http://goldcoastairport.com.au/ and is on the border of NSW and Queensland states. It operates direct domestic flights and a few Asian and New Zealand connections. The airport is closed in the night. The GCA is directly connected to Surfers Paradise and many major hotels through the Gold Coast Tourist Shuttle - http://gcshuttle.com.au/ that offers a number of package offers for visiting tourists.

Sunshine Coast is located 80 km north of Brisbane and is served directly by the small Sunshine Coast Airport (IATA: MCY) - http://www.sunshinecoastairport.com.au/ with limited flights to Australian east coast cities and some seasonal flights to neighbouring New Zealand. The public bus stop connecting the airport to the Sunshine Coast towns is about 1 km from the terminal. Shuttle services operated by Henry's, cost about $20 for a hotel drop. Taxis and rental cars are also available in abundance at the terminals.

Both Gold Coast and Sunshine Coast have multiple bus and train connections from Brisbane.

For those visiting Gold Coast and Sunshine Coast, the best option is to see the place by foot or book a rental car. Taxis and bicycles are also available. Gold Coast has a public bus service by Surfside Buslines - http://www.surfside.com.au/ that operates 24 hrs daily.

🌏 Weather & Best Time to Visit

Brisbane, Gold Coast and the Sunshine Coast have a humid subtropical climate with dry moderately warm winters and hot and humid summers. Located in the southern hemisphere, winters are during the middle of the year and summertime between December and March. Winter temperatures between May and September see an average high of about 21 degrees Celsius and lows around 11 degrees.

Summer temperatures between November and March see an average high of about 28 degrees Celsius and low of 20 degrees. These are also the wettest months averaging at least 150mm of monthly rainfall. The dry weather and mild temperature make the winter months

the ideal time to visit this region.

Sights & Activities: What to See & Do

🌐 Fortitude Valley

Located just a km from the Brisbane CBD, Fortitude

Valley is regarded as one of the primary hubs of Brisbane

nightlife and adult entertainment. This cultural core of the

city is home to innumerable restaurants, bars, clubs,

malls, and the Brisbane Chinatown.

It is often recommended to start the walk of the Valley at the Brunswick Mall on Brunswick Street at the city end, a popular meeting point for locals and visitors alike. The place is famous for the McWhirters food hall and plenty of cafés and restaurants. Running parallel to Brunswick Street Mall is the Chinatown Mall – the central hub of the city's Chinatown that welcomes every visitor with the typical Chinese arched gate. Walking up the street takes one to the shopping precinct with the iconic Dooley's Irish Pub.

There are a number of annual events that are home to the Fortitude Valley. The 3-day Valley Fiesta lives up to its name with numerous live concerts, food stalls, and market stalls. Local and neighbouring artists, restaurants, and vendors participate in this fiesta. Jazz lovers have a treat with the 5-day biennial International Jazz Festival in early June. The Straight Out Of Brisbane is an event highlighting the independent art scene of the city with exhibitions, performances, screenings, live art, and live music. The Big Gay Day event by the LGBT community raises money through many day long events that include concerts and drag shows.

Fortitude Valley has a number of must-visit bars and clubs including the Cloudland restaurant and the multi award winning Cru Bar and Cellar. The Press Club is popular for its live music and stunning interior décor. It has free entry and is open from 7 in the evening.

🌐 King George Square & Brisbane City Hall

Located between Ann Street and Adelaide Street in Brisbane is the King George Square. Built in the first quarter of the 20th century, this public square was originally a market square and was called the Albert Square; today this open square is home to the Brisbane City Hall. The square was widened and renamed in 1936 after the death of King George V and a statue was installed of the departed king. The statue of King George riding his horse stands in front of the City Hall. The square is guarded by 2 brass lions along with statues of eminent Queenslanders at the Speaker's Corner of the square.

The Brisbane City Hall is a heritage listed building that was built in the 1920s. Witness and backdrop to many social, cultural, and civic events, the City Hall was rededicated to the Queenslanders with its reopening in 2013 after a staggering $215 million 3-year restoration program. This iconic building is a major city landmark and is listed by the National Trust of Queensland and the Queensland Heritage Register as a 'culturally, historically and architecturally significant building'. With its present restoration, the City Hall can host events accommodating up to 2500 guests.

The foundation and the building of the City Hall was an interesting chronology of events. The first foundation stone was laid in 1917. The hollow foundation stone contained a zinc cylinder time capsule with copies of the city newspaper, copy of the Incorporation and Proclamation of the City, a copy of City Council meeting, some coins, and a message from the Governor. This first foundation stone was found out of alignment in 1935 after the construction of the City Hall on the second foundation stone laid in 1920! The original foundation stone, once claimed to be in the City Council Depot was later declared as lost.

The City Hall, designed in an Italian Renaissance style with Corinthian columns, was the tallest building in the city when it was opened in 1930. The 70m high clock tower with 4 clock faces are the largest clock faces in the country with the diameter of the dial measuring 5m. The observation platform above the clock tower is open to the public seven days a week and offers spectacular views of the city.

The City Hall is open 8:00 am to 5:00 pm (opens at 9:00 am on weekends and public holidays) and has free guided tours between 10:30 am and 3:30 pm. The observation platform is open from 10:00 am to 5:00 pm. Other than the beautifully restored auditoriums and lounges, the City Hall houses the Museum of Brisbane and two cafes – Red Cross Café and Shingle Inn. It hosts a number of concerts, exhibitions, and conferences throughout the year.

Cathedral of St Stephen

249 Elizabeth Street

Brisbane

QLD 4001

Tel: +61 7 3336 9111

http://www.cathedralofststephen.org.au/

Built in a Gothic Revival style of architecture, the Cathedral of St Stephen was built between 1864 and 1922 and has a Roman Catholic affiliation. The foundation stone was laid by Bishop Quinn on St Stephen's Feast in 1863 with a vision to build a grand ornate church. However, the economic depression in the late 19th century not only delayed the construction of the church, it also downsized it to a third of the original plan. It was solemnized in 1874. A decade later, the façade was enriched with marble and stained glass. Major restoration and extension of the cathedral was completed in as late as 1989 and it was consecrated on December 4th, 1989.

The floor plan of the cathedral is laid out in a crucifix shape. The cathedral is predominantly made from

Brisbane tuff and the Blessed Sacrament Church from reinforced concrete. It has spire topped sandstone towers and windows with stained glass imported from Munich. The lightweight plastered ceilings in the interior are supported by milk-white columns that bring a serene ambience to the nave.

The cathedral is located within a 10 minute walk from the Central Station. It is open for tours on Sundays at 9:00 am, 11:00 am, and 1:00 pm and on weekdays at 10:30 am after Mass. The cathedral also hosts a number of choirs throughout the year, details of which are posted on the website.

🌐 South Bank

The South Bank precinct in Brisbane, aptly named for its location on the southern banks of the River Brisbane, is an educational, cultural, and recreational hub and has a number of notable attractions.

The South Bank Parklands is not only the biggest tourist attraction of South Banks; it is also one of the biggest in the state, attracting an estimated 11 million visitors every year. Located directly opposite the Brisbane CBD, it is connected by the Victoria Bridge and the Goodwill Bridge. The most dominating landmark is the Wheel of Brisbane Ferris Wheel. The Parklands has a beautifully decorated Arbour with bouganvilleas and cobbled pathways. Other places of interest in the Parklands include the Nepal

Peace Pagoda, the 2000-seat Courier Mail Piazza open-air amphitheatre, and the multi award winning man-made Streets Beach. The Parklands has a number of cafes and restaurants and hosts many popular festivals throughout the year.

Another major attraction is the Queensland Cultural Centre (QCC), a popular multi-venue centre. Located in the QCC is the Queensland Art Gallery - http://www.qagoma.qld.gov.au/, established in 1895. This museum and art gallery is dedicated to profiling Indigenous art of Australia and is also known worldwide for its innovative learning programs for children. It has some important artworks including the 1905 La Belle Hollandaise by Picasso. It is open 7 days a week. The Queensland Gallery of Modern Art is the largest gallery of contemporary and modern art in Australia, having attracted over a million visitors within 4 years of its opening in 2006. The Queensland Performing Arts Centre which opened in the 1970s now houses 4 different theatres with a total seating capacity of nearly 5000 and hosts a variety of performances – orchestra, ballet, comedy, musical, theatre, and cabaret. The Queensland Museum – originally established in 1862 – was made a part of the QCC in 1986.

The Museum has some fascinating displays and exhibitions on the history of Queensland and Australia, the Aboriginal people of the region, and the various modes of transport over the years. The QCC also houses the State Library of Queensland. The library, established in 1896, is now housed in an architecture award winning building, and contains many important collections. There are free tours of the buildings for the general public.

Other places of tourist interest in South Banks include the Queensland Maritime Museum - located near the Goodwill Bridge - that has two levels of displays from the maritime history of the region. Little Stanley Street and Grey Street are popular with the myriad of restaurants, cafes, and shopping boutiques. These streets also have a number of heritage listed buildings.

🌏 Roma Street Parkland

16 hectares of subtropical garden at the heart of the city makes the Roma Street Parkland the largest of its kind in the world. Easily accessible through the historic Roma Street Station, the parkland is adjacent to the Brisbane

Transit Centre. Cradled amidst the web of boardwalks and pathways, the Roma Street Parkland features a wide variety of recreational parks and themed gardens. With rocky outcrops, cascading waterways, and many artworks by local artists, it is a paradise amidst the busy concrete jungle.

The area was originally a place for meetings and ceremonies of the local people. Being a part of the original settlement area of the city, the Roma Street Station was constructed in 1875. The terminal was extensively used to carry war materials and personnel in the World War II. The importance of the station grew manifold and it was developed as a hub for the metropolitan and long-distance train network. Although commercial freight handling is no more done at the Roma

Street Station, it remains an important terminal in the city, both for locals and visitors.

The parkland area was developed to its present form and opened to the public in 2001 and has since provided a much needed relief in the city's landscape. The parkland is still the home of an open-air amphitheatre – previously known as the Albert Amphitheatre as the park was called the Albert Park. Many theatre productions and orchestral concerts are hosted in this amphitheatre. The parkland also has free tours by volunteer guides. It is open throughout the day every day.

🌐 Lone Pine Koala Sanctuary

708 Jesmond Road

Fig Tree Pocket

QLD 4069

Tel: +61 7 3378 1366

http://www.koala.net/

Named after the lone hoop pine (also known as the Queensland pine), the Lone Pine Koala Sanctuary is the oldest and largest koala sanctuary in the world, having been founded in 1927. Spread over 4.6 hectares, the sanctuary started with two koalas – Jack and Jill. Today it is the home to 130 koalas along with many kangaroos, wombats, dingoes, and other Australian native animals.

The sanctuary is one of a kind in the world and is the perfect place for a visit by the whole family. It is one of the very few sanctuaries where one can hold a koala – for a fee. There are strict rules for the maintenance of the koalas and no koala is held for more than 30 minutes in the whole day. The 2 hectare kangaroo reserve is where one can pet and feed the free roaming kangaroos.

The sanctuary also has a large collection of birds including cockatoos, lorikeets, emus, kookaburras, and Australian parrots. Once every day, there is an exciting show by the birds of prey displaying their agility and keen eyesight. Visitors are also treated to the Sheep Dog Shows and feeding of the lorikeets.

🌏 Gold Coast Beach Resorts

Gold Coast is known for its beautiful and unique beaches and foreshores. The place attracts millions of visitors every year with its innumerable beaches that stretch from Couran Cove to Rainbow Bay.

Surfers Paradise

http://www.surfersparadise.com

The iconic Surfers Paradise is a suburb in the Gold Coast that has developed to one of the foremost coast-destinations of Australia attracting tourist from different parts of the globe including Japan, England, China, and the USA. The area was first identified in the late 19th century but rose into prominence in the 2nd half of the 20th century. A real estate boom with stunning hotels and many skyscrapers along with 3 km of pristine sandy beaches made it one of the most loved tourist destinations of the country. 'Surfers' – as it is known locally – also has a number of heritage-listed buildings. Equipped with water safaris, theme parks, hot air balloons, state-of-the-art theatres, a wide range of restaurants, and an exceptionally vibrant nightlife, Surfers is able to cater to visitors of every taste. The 4-weekend long Surfers Paradise Festival celebrates the art, culture, and cuisine of the region through many family events, markets, exhibitions, and concerts. A must-visit is the Beachfront Markets – a perfect place for bargain hunters with free live entertainment by street performers, setting up the perfect holiday backdrop.

Main Beach

With al fresco dining, chic shopping boutiques, and a stylish beachside area, Main Beach is the place to be for the ones who want to splurge. The walk from the Surfers Paradise to the Main Beach is one of the best coastal walks in the region with beautiful sandy beaches and the stunningly 'wealthy skyline'. The place gets crowded during the evenings and weekends especially along the beach and the Tedder Avenue with fine dining restaurants and modern cafes. The Spit, located to the north of the Main Beach, has the famous Palazzo Versace Hotel, Marina Mirage Shopping and Dining Centre, and the Sea World. Main Beach also offers some unique experiences for the visitors including the Rivers Lunch Cruise (Tel: 5527 6361) – an exotic international cuisine lunch and sightseeing aboard the Voyager yacht.

Broadbeach

Broadbeach is a suburb of the Gold Coast that is popular for its wide expanse of sand beaches and the adjoining parklands. Low rise structures, canal waterways and a number of parks alongside the beach area make it one of the most pristine and natural coastal destinations of this island nation. Broadbeach is also regarded as a Mecca for dining with its myriad of gourmet delis, brasseries, and champagne salons. Entertainment is a 24-hr activity in Broadbeach with numerous world class lounges and bars. Festivals and community events along with street musicians and dancers provide amusement to adults and children alike. Shopaholics have a field day at the Pacific Fair, one of the largest retail centres in Australia with over 300 stores. For the bargain hunters, there is the Friday night Lantern-Lit Market and the bi-monthly Kurrawa Park beachfront markets.

Burleigh Heads

http://www.goldcoastburleightourism.com.au

BRISBANE, GOLD COAST & SUNSHINE COAST TRAVEL GUIDE

Located between Coolangatta and Surfers Paradise, Burleigh Heads is a Gold Coast suburb popular for its surf break, numerous shopping centres, fabulous scenery, and a warm vibrancy that goes up a few notches on the weekends with street performers, barbeques, and dance sessions. The patrolled beaches of Burleigh are lined with natural parklands and dotted with picnic spots. There are also many opportunities for al fresco dining, especially at James Street. James Street, with the perfect feel of a seaside village straight out of the movies, also has a number of stores selling souvenirs and local products.

With barbeques, surfing, beach cricket, fire-twirlers, and local music, the Burleigh headland, popularly called 'The Point', is a must-visit attraction in the evenings and weekends. West Burleigh is known for being a shopping

Mecca although there a number of local weekend markets that have a substantial patronage.

Held on the last Sunday every month, the Burleigh 'Arts and Crafts' Market is popular for Australian made products. The Village Markets on the 1st and 3rd Sundays every month is popular for its alternative and vintage collections.

With many opportunities for bird watching along with the presence of the Burleigh Head National Park and the David Fleay National Park, even the nature lovers have something for them at Burleigh.

🌏 Gold Coast Hinterland

Located inland from the coastal strip of Gold Coast, the Hinterland is home to many national parks, lush rainforest, bush walks, local wineries, and quaint communities. Contradicting the hustle and bustle of the tourist spots, the Hinterland is one of the best kept secrets of the region that transforms a visitor to the peace and tranquility of nature.

There are a number of regions that make up the Hinterland. The Tweed Range is the western extension of the pre-historic Tweed Volcano that once spanned over 100 sq km! The smaller Nimmel Range is home to the 489m high Mt Nimmel and the only access point to the picturesque Springbook Mountain. The Tamborine Mountain region spans 28 sq km and is popular for its walking tracks, waterfalls, and art galleries of the locals. Regarded as one of the most beautiful in the state, the Numbinah Valley region has many rainforest walks, waterfalls, rocky outcrops, and cleared grazing lands. Largely undeveloped, the valley brings one face to face with the mysticism and beauty of nature.

🌐 Caloundra

Located 90 km north of Brisbane, Caloundra is the southernmost community in the Sunshine Coast that is known for its beaches and its old-fashioned charm. Caloundra is very well connected by rail and road from the neighbouring cities and towns. The nearest train station is Landsborough in the Sunshine Coast Hinterland.

Originally discovered in the late 19th century, the region became popular within a short time due to its proximity to the beaches. It was a major defense base for Australia in

World War II for its strategic position. Today, Caloundra, surrounded by the Rainforest Drive, Currimundi Creek, Beerwah State Forest, Pumicestone Channel, and the Pacific Ocean, is primarily an amalgamation of beaches that have earned the reputation as some of the best beaches of Queensland. Amongst the popular beaches are the strictly patrolled beaches of Bulcock and King's. Shelley Beach and Dickie Beach are popular with families for the picnic spots and rock pools.

The more adventurous head for the Golden Beach where one can engage in windsurfing, kayaking, and surf-skiing. The award winning Sunshine Coast Skydivers - http://www.sunshinecoastskydivers.com.au operates Australia's highest skydives. There are a number of tours in Caloundra including the eco-exploring Caloundra Cruise and Chartered Scenic Flight Tour. Storeyline Tours

- http://www.storeylinetours.com.au/ offers Day Tours to the neighbouring villages, hinterland, and wineries.

🌏 Noosa

Located 136 km north of Brisbane in the Sunshine Coast, Noosa is a popular tourist attraction of Queensland for its shady beaches, up-market shopping, and scenic beauty. It has a number of suburbs with Noosa Heads being the primary tourist area with Noosa Spit, Noosa Woods, and the Noosa National Park.

Noosa is connected from the Brisbane Airport and the Sunshine Coast Airport by bus, shuttle, and taxi service. Greyhound Bus service has multiple daily connections to Noosa. For those opting for the train, Noosa is accessible from a number of stations – Cooroy, Eumundi,

Maryborough, Nambour, and Pomona. Within the city, one can use the Translink buses.

The main attraction of Noosa is certainly the beaches coupled with perfect surfing conditions. Along with the annual Noosa Festival of Surfing, Noosa has hosted many prestigious surfing competitions. Noosa is also one of the foremost kite surfing destinations in the world; novices and the curious can even take basic lessons at - http://noosakitesurfing.com/ in kite surfing before taking flight. Noosa is also close to the Fraser Island – the largest sand island in the world. Another attraction of Noosa is the koalas in the Noosa National Park. On the other hand, the Noosa Lions Park near the Weyba Creek attracts visitors and locals alike with its various festivals and concerts. It also hosts the popular Noosa International Food and Wine Festival.

🌏 Maroochydore

Located along the southern border of the Sunshine Coast Airport, Maroochydore is a popular commercial urban area and is a central point with easy access to many of Queensland's popular tourist resorts. It is named after the red-billed black swan – Muru-kutchi in Aboriginal indigenous language – which is commonly sighted here, Maroochydore is known as a major venue for surfing carnivals and the Sunshine Castle in Bli Bli.

The hamlet of Bli Bli, located a few km inland from Maroochydore was once the hub of the sugar cane industry. From the 1970s, it has become a tourist attraction for the fairy-tale Sunshine Castle -

http://www.sunshinecastle.com/.

Built in the Norman architectural style, this exciting and

unique landmark has medieval additions like moats,

towers, turrets, and a drawbridge. Actors dressed as

knights and medieval merchants not only entertain the

crowd, they also offer lessons in sword fighting. Castle

Walks and Treasure Hunts engage the old and the young

alike. There is a Castle Store where one can buy mock

medieval swords and clothes. From 1986 onwards, a

private doll collection was purchased and is displayed in

the Toy and Doll Museum. The Castle Café has a range

of offerings from the medieval lamb shanks to the modern

cup of coffee. The Castle is open every day (except

Christmas Day) from 9:30 am to 4:30 pm and has an

entrance fee of $14 for an adult ($10 for children between

10 & 15 yrs).

Budget Tips

 # Accommodation

City Palms Motel

55 Brunswick Street

Fortitude Valley

QLD 4006

Tel: 1 800 655 381 (toll free)

http://www.citypalmsmotel.com

Located about a 15-minutes walk from the Brisbane CBD, the 3-star City Palms Motel is close to the city attractions and yet provides a calm and relaxing ambience.

This smoke-free property has nearby parking and has free Wi-Fi in its premises. It has multilingual staff. There is an outdoor space with barbeque facilities.

The 37 air-conditioned rooms have various facilities – like garden view, microwave, ironing board, etc. - depending on the room categories. Room rates start from $89 for an ensuite double room.

Ellie's Guest House

124 Methyr Road

New Farm,

Brisbane, QLD

Tel: 0418 188 918

http://elliesguesthouse.com.au/

Located close to the Brisbane River adjacent to the

Brisbane Powerhouse, Ellie's Guest House offers homely

accommodations in a beautiful old-charm woodhouse.

There is free parking. This no-frills guest house has free

towels and laundry facilities.

All rooms are equipped with a kitchenette with a fridge,

sink, and other basic kitchen amenities. The ensuite

rooms are either single bed, double bed, or with bunk beds. Room rates start from $44.

Paramount Motel

649 Main Street

Kangaroo Point

Brisbane, QLD 4169

Tel: 07 3393 1444

http://www.paramountmotel.com.au

Located hardly 2 km from the heart of Brisbane and a short ferry ride to the CBD, Paramount Motel promises a quiet and enjoyable experience at an affordable price. There is free parking and Wi-Fi. There is a pool and a barbeque. Non smoking rooms are available and some also come with a kitchenette. Family rooms are available.

Room rates start from $110 per night for single or double room, and from $175 for a family room (4 – 6 guests).

International Beach Resort

84 The Esplanade

Surfers Paradise

QLD 4217

Tel: 07 5539 0099

http://www.internationalresort.com.au

This sea-front high-rise hotel has 120 air-conditioned rooms with a sea view. Limited free parking is available. The property has a recreation area and a pool. Facilities include ATM banking, sauna, spa, and a safe deposit box near the reception area. There is also a travel desk. There is also a café, restaurant, and a poolside bar.

Rooms range from studios to 2 bedroom apartments. Room rates start from $99 per night.

River Esplanade Motel

98 River Esplanade

Mooloolaba, Sunshine Coast

QLD 4557

Tel: 07 5444 3855

http://www.riveresplanade.com.au/

Located close to the Underwater World and adjacent to the beach, River Esplanade Motel offers 21 air-conditioned rooms in a cozy ambience. There is free parking and Wi-Fi at a surcharge. There is an open

garden space and a pool. Dry cleaning and laundry

services are available.

The ensuite rooms come with LCD TV and hair dryers.

Room rates start from $95 with a minimum stay of 2

nights.

 Places to Eat

The Spice Avenue Balti Restaurant

Shop 12, 190 Birkdale

Brisbane QLD 4159

Tel: 07 3822 9822

http://www.thespiceavenue.com.au/

Serving British Indian and Bangladeshi cuisine, the Australian branch of The Spice Avenue has won the hearts of many with their spicy and delicious dishes. Fried starters of different kinds start from $6 and main curry dishes start from $25. There is a wide range of sauce/curries to choose from, from the mildly spicy to the burning hot. Vegetarian dishes are priced around $17. It has a full-license bar and serves a wide variety of wines, spirits, and beers.

Azafran Restaurant

97 Ekbin Road

Annerly

Brisbane QLD4103

Tel: 07 3892 1776

http://www.azafran.com.au

Serving Australian cuisine ranging from breakfast and brunch to late night fine dining, Azafran restaurant has made a name for itself with excellent service, great food, and cozy atmosphere. The menu is updated seasonally based on the best available produce in the market. Vegetarian starters start from $8. Seafood and goose liver entrees are priced from $20. Main dishes of duck, lamb, or chicken are priced about $35. A 5-course set meal is available for $75 without wine and at $125 with matching wines.

Reserve Restaurant Milton

Cnr Coronation Drive & Park Road

Brisbane QLD 4064

Tel: 07 3368 1314

http://www.reserverestaurant.com.au/milton.html

Housed in the heritage-listed Cook Terrace Building, this award-winning restaurant offers an elegant setting for an intimate dinner or a drink at the Champagne Bar. Using the best available local produce, the restaurant serves contemporary European cuisine with a French influence. Vegetarian, chicken, and rabbit meat entrees are priced between $17 and $25.

Main dishes are priced around $38 and includes lamb, pork, beef, duck, and venison. Pre-fixed lunch menus are also available – 2-course at $29.50.

Bazaar at the QT Hotel

7 Staghom Avenue

Surfers Paradise

QLD 4217

Tel: 07 5584 1200

http://www.qtgoldcoast.com.au/food-drink/bazaar/

This busy and bustling restaurant serves international cuisine buffet. With a floor to ceiling glass partition, guests are treated to a view of the kitchen while the food is being prepared. There is a dress code as no bare feet and males wearing sleeveless tops are allowed. There is a great and elaborate selection of dishes in the buffet. Breakfast (6:30 am to 10:30 am) for an adult is priced at

$69, Sunday Lunch (12noon to 3:00 pm) at $59, and

Dinner (5:30 pm to 9:00 pm) at $69.

Karma Waters

Shop 5, 7 Venning Street

Mooloolaba, QLD 4557

Tel: 07 5452 6722

http://karmawatersrestaurant.com.au

Open both days and nights on all 7 days, the Karma

Waters is a restaurant serving Portuguese cuisine.

Excellent staff with prompt service coupled with delicious

food has brought in great reviews for this restaurant.

Breakfast for an adult costs about $20. Wraps and

meatball preparations for lunch are priced around $20.

Main dishes in the dinner menu are priced between $25 and $30 and has a wide variety of fish and meat items.

 Shopping

West End

Brisbane

Named after West End in London, the area is known for its restaurants and cafes, and for the variety in shopping. Shops are concentrated along the Boundary Street. Other than the ethnic stores and organic grocery stores, West End hosts a Saturday Farmer's Market which is one of the largest in the greater Brisbane area.

Noosa Farmer's Market

Sunshine Coast

Located on Weyba Road, this flea market sells high quality local produce at a very affordable price. From baked goods to local seafood, and from Asian street food to gourmet meats, the market has a wide range of products. There are many options for breakfast and coffee. This market is a great place to buy local cheese and olives.

The City – Queen Street Mall

Queen St

Brisbane, QLD 4000

http://www.bnecity.com.au/

Located in Queen Street, this mall is regarded as one of the premier shopping destinations in the state. It has 6 shopping centres with over 1000 stores housing over 250 local and international brands. It attracts over a staggering 26 million visitors annually! Located close to the city attractions, the mall itself has developed into an attraction for the visitors and locals alike for its huge array of offerings.

Centro Surfers Paradise

Surfers Paradise, Gold Coast

http://www.centrosurfersparadise.com.au

Located on Cavall Avenue, the shopping centre is not only frequented by locals but also the visitors to buy the essentials. Other than the variety of shops which include curios and souvenir stores, one may also catch live performances on special occasions. There is also a popular kid's zone. Although the branded stores close by 5:00 pm, the shopping centre along with the supermarket is open until 10:00 pm. The centre is open all 7 days.

Brisbane Arcade

http://www.brisbanearcade.com.au/

Located between Adelaide Street and Queen Street, the arcade is a narrow strip that acts as a pass connecting the 2 streets. Home to many unique stores including clothing, jewelry, fashion, gifts, food, watches, and antiques, the Brisbane Arcade is one the few remaining heritage shopping arcades of the city, having a history of nearly a 100 years. It is open from 9:00 am to 5:00 pm every day with extended closing hours on Fridays (8:00 pm).

Know Before You Go

🌐 Entry Requirements

With the exception of New Zealand, nationals of most countries will need a valid passport and a visa when travelling to Australia. Upon arrival, you will also be required to fill out a passenger card, which includes a declaration regarding your health and character. A tourist visa is usually valid for 6 months, but can be extended for another 6 months. If travelling to Australia for business reasons, you will want to look into the requirements for a short term or long term business visas. The former is valid for up to 3 months, while the latter is valid for up to 4 years, but requires sponsorship from an Australian company.

🌐 Health Insurance

If visiting Australia from a country that has a reciprocal health care agreement with Australia, you will be able to use Medicare - Australia's public health insurance - for the duration of your stay. Participating countries include Ireland, New Zealand,

Italy, Sweden, Norway, Slovenia, Belgium, Finland, the Netherlands and the UK. However, this only covers emergency care and limits you to using public hospitals. Visitors on a student visa from Norway, Finland, Malta and the Republic of Ireland may require additional cover and visitors who do not have access to Medicare will be required, as part of their visa application, to obtain adequate healthcare for the duration of their stay in Australia. To extend your cover, Overseas Visitors Health Cover (OVHC) can be arranged through a number of Australian health fund companies. Additional health insurance is mandatory if visiting on a long stay working visa. There are no required vaccinations for entering Australia, but a booster shot for tetanus and diphtheria will be a good idea, if your last vaccination was more than ten years ago. If travelling from Southeast Asia, you may want to get a shot for Hepatitis A and B, as well as typhoid.

Travelling with Pets

Nearly all dogs and cats travelling to Australia will need to spend some time in quarantine, but the duration depends on the country of origin. The only countries exempt from this requirement is New Zealand, Cocos Island and Norfolk Island.

The minimum quarantine period is 10 days and to qualify for this, your pet will need to be tested for rabies 6 months prior to your travel date. The cost for quarantine and customs clearance is approximately $1,800AUD. You will need to apply for an import permit for your pet. If travelling from a non-approved country such as Russia, India, Sri Lanka and the Philippines, your pet will need to spend 6 months in an approved country and be tested for rabies prior to being allowed entry in Australia. Approved countries include Antigua & Barbuda, Argentina, Austria, the Bahamas, Belgium, Bermuda, the British Virgin Islands, Brunei, Bulgaria, Canada, the Canary and Balearic Islands, the Cayman Islands, Chile, the Republic of Croatia, the Republic of Cyprus, the Czech Republic, Denmark, Finland, France, Germany, Gibraltar, Greece, Greenland, Guernsey, Hong Kong, Hungary, Ireland, the Isle of Man, Israel, Italy, Jamaica, Jersey, Kuwait, Latvia, Lithuania, Luxembourg, Macau, Malta, parts of Malaysia (Peninsular, Sabah and Sarawak only), Monaco, Montenegro, the Netherlands, Netherlands—Antilles & Aruba, Norway, Poland, Portugal, Puerto Rico, Qatar, Reunion, Saipan, Serbia, Seychelles, Slovakia, Slovenia, South Africa, South Korea, Spain, St Kitts and Nevis, St Lucia, St Vincent & the Grenadines, Sweden, Switzerland (including Liechtenstein), Taiwan, Trinidad and Tobago, the United Arab Emirates, the

United Kingdom, the United States, Northern Mariana Islands, Puerto Rico and the US Virgin Islands as well as American Samoa, Bahrain, Barbados, Christmas Island, Cook Island, the Falkland Islands, the Federated States of Micronesia, Fiji, French Polynesia, Guam, Hawaii, Iceland, Japan, Kiribati Mauritius, Nauru, New Caledonia, Niue, Palau, Papua New Guinea, Samoa, Singapore, the Solomon Islands, the Kingdom of Tonga, Tuvalu, Vanuatu and the Futuna Islands. There are quarantine stations in Sydney and Melbourne. A quarantine period can be waived in the case of service dog, provided that proper documented evidence of the dog's status is submitted, but in this case, the dog will need to be inspected upon arrival by an approved veterinarian and supervised for the 10 day period immediately after entry. You are not allowed to bring certain dog breeds such as the Dogo Argentino, Fila Brazileiro, Japanese Tosa, Pit Bull Terrier, American Pit Bull, Perro de Presa Canario or Presa Canario into Australia. Other animals that cannot be brought into Australia are chinchillas, fish, ferrets, guinea pigs, hamsters, lizards, mice, snakes, spiders and turtles. In the case of avian species, only birds originating from New Zealand are allowed.

🌏 Airports

Sydney Airport (SYD) is located just 8km south of Sydney's central business district and serves as the primary gateway for international air traffic into Australia. It is the country's busiest airport and provides connections to New Zealand, Singapore, Hong Kong, Dubai, Japan, the USA and Malaysia. Domestically, it also provides access to the country's six main states, as well as to Tasmania. The second busiest airport is **Melbourne Airport** (MEL). It is located about 23km from the central business area of Melbourne, but this is easy to reach via the Skybus Super Shuttle, which connects to the city's public transport network at the Southern Cross station. Melbourne Airport welcomes international flights from the Far East, the Middle East and the USA and also connects to Australia's top domestic destinations. The busiest airport in Queensland is **Brisbane Airport** (BNE), which provides connections to over 40 domestic destinations and over 25 international destinations. Other important airports in Queensland are the **Gold Coast Airport** (OOL) and the **Cairns Airport** (CNS). As the 4th busiest airport, **Perth Airport** (PER) serves as a gateway to Western Australia. **Adelaide Airport** (ADL) is the most important airport in the Southern Territory of Australia, while **Darwin Airport** (DRW), one of the oldest airports in Australia, opens up the Northern Territory. **Canberra Airport** (CBR) provides access to the capital. Tasmania is served by **Hobart International Airport** (HBA) in Hobart.

Airlines

Qantas Airways is the third oldest airline in the world. It was founded in 1920 through the efforts of two Australian Flying Corps veterans, W Hudson Fysh and Paul McGinness. The enterprise pioneered a series of milestones, starting with the establishment of an airmail service, the Flying Doctor Service, a regular connection between Brisbane and Darwin and the addition of international destinations such as Singapore. Qantas was an early adapter to the benefits of Boeing jumbo jets and one of the first airlines to establish a trans-Pacific route. Today it is Australia's national flag carrier and the country's largest airline. Qantas is a partner of the OneWorld Air Alliance, connecting it with British Airlines, Iberia, Japan Airlines, Finnair, LAN Airlines and Sri Lankan Airlines.

Qantas has a founding interest in Australia's budget service, Jetstar Airways, which is based at Melbourne Airport. Together with Qantas, Jetstar oversees Jetstar Asia Airways, Jetstar

Pacific Airlines and Jetstar Japan. Qantas also operates a regional brand, QantasLink, which harnesses the combined coverage of Eastern Australian Airlines, Sunstate Airlines and Southern Australia Airlines to provide a regional and domestic service. Eastern Australia Airlines was founded late in the 1940s, when it served mainly to connect remote rural communities under the name Tamair. During the mid-1980s, it was acquired by Australian Airlines, who in turn sold it to Qantas in 1992.

After Qantas, Virgin Australia is the second largest airline. Founded under the Virgin brand by Richard Branson and Brett Godfrey in 2000, the company expanded rapidly after September 2001 to fill the gap left by the demise of Ansett Australia. Virgin Australia is in partnership with the regional service SkyWest Airlines as well as Air New Zealand and the US carrier Delta. Additionally, it operates the budget airline, Tigerair Australia as a subsidiary of Virgin Australia. Tigerair offers connections to 11 domestic destinations as well as nearby Bali.

West Wing Aviation is a domestic service based in Queensland and manages connections to smaller and more remote destinations within Queensland. Airnorth was founded in the late 1970s. Based in Darwin, it provides a regional service that covers the northern part of Australia. King Island Airlines offers connections between Moorabbin, near Melbourne and King Island, Tasmania.

🌏 Hubs

Sydney Airport serves as the primary hub for Qantas Air. Qantas also uses Melbourne Airport, Brisbane Airport, Perth Airport and Adelaide Airport as hubs. Virgin Australia uses Brisbane Airport, Melbourne Airport and Sydney Airport as hubs, but also has a strong presence at Adelaide Airport, Perth Airport and Gold Coast Airport. Additionally, Melbourne Airport serves as hub for the Virgin subsidiary Tigerair, as well as Jetstar Airlines. Darwin International Airport serves as a primary hub for Airnorth. West Wing Aviation uses Townsville Airport in Queensland as hub. Brisbane Airport serves as a hub for Sunstate Airlines.

🌐 Money Matters

🌐 Currency

The currency of Australia is the Australian dollar. Notes are issued in denominations of $5, $10, $20, $50 and $100. Coins are issued in denominations of 5 cents, 10 cents, 20 cents and 50 cents as well as $1 and $2.

🌐 Banking/ATMs

ATM machines are widely distributed across Australia in both urban and rural locations. Besides bank lobbies, they are often found in shopping centers, service stations, convenience stores and pubs. You should be able to use bank cards that are part of the Cirrus, Plus or Maestro networks. Most ATMs will explicitly indicate which cards are accepted. Using a debit card is fairly easy in Australia, but many ATMs will charge an additional fee of $2 or more for non-customers. There are exceptions. As the Westpac banking group is partnered with several overseas banks including Bank of America, Scotia Bank and Barclays, customers of those banks will be exempted from the banking fee. An alternative to using your bank card is the

Travelex Cash Passport, an easy-to-use prepaid card which can be topped up using your debit card.

Credit Cards

MasterCard and Visa are widely accepted throughout Australia, while Diners Club and American Express will also be legal tender at larger shops and chain stores. Some shops will decline credit cards for purchases under AUS$15 and surcharges may apply for some businesses. Until recently, credit card users in Australia had the choice of using a PIN or signature as security for credit card transactions, but from August 2016, PIN-enabled cards will be mandatory. You should make sure that your credit card is compatible with this new policy. Also remember to advise your bank or credit card of your travel plans prior to your departure.

Tourist Tax

From July 2016, working backpackers will be taxed at 32.5 percent on their Australian income.

🌏 Claiming Back VAT

Visitors to Australia can obtain a refund on purchases of at least $300, spent at a single business. Residents of the Australia's External Territories - the Norfolk Islands, Christmas Island and the Cocos (Keeling) Islands - also qualify for a refund from GST paid under the Tourist Refund Scheme (TRS). To obtain a refund, you must present valid documentation of your purchases in the form of a tax invoice or sales receipt at an international airport or seaport when departing Australia and this should happen within 60 days of making those purchases. You should keep the goods handy within your hand luggage, to have it available for inspection. To save time, download the TRS app where you can enter details electronically and use a specially dedicated shortcut queue to process your claim.

🌏 Tipping Policy

In Australia, restaurants are required by law to pay their waiting staff a working wage and tipping is not really expected, although the influence of tourism as well as American culture has influenced Australian attitudes in recent years. In high-end restaurants, roughly half of the diners might be expected to leave a tip and in big cities, it will be more common to tip. If service is good and you want to show your appreciation, 10 percent is regarded as fair and sufficient. It is not common practice to tip in hotels and in casinos, tipping is forbidden. In bars, it is accepted practice to tell the bartender to keep the change. The same applies to cab drivers.

 Connectivity

Mobile Phones

Australia uses the GSM mobile network, which means that it should be compatible with phones from the UK or the European Union, but may be incompatible with phones from the USA and Canada. If you are able to use Australian networks, you will still face the high charges levied for international roaming. There is an alternative. If your phone is unlocked, you will be able to replace your own SIM card with an Australian SIM card for the duration of your stay.

Australia has 3 basic mobile networks - Telstra, Vodafone and Optus. Telstra offers the best coverage of Australia's rural and more remote locations, but is also one of the more expensive operators. If you plan to stick to urban locations, the coverage offered by Optus and Vodafone might be sufficient for your needs. Telstra sim cards are available at $2, with recharge packages starting at $20. Data only packages are priced at between $30 and $50. Optus sim cards begin at $2 for just the sim, with top-ups priced at between $10 and $50. Vodafone pre-paid sim cards begin at $1 for just the sim, with data packages priced at between $3 and $15. For a super budget option, consider the deals offered by the reseller Amaysim, which also offers the option to pay for top-ups online, via PayPal.

Dialling Code

The dialling code for Australia is +61.

Emergency Numbers

General emergency: 000

Text Emergency Relay Service: 106

MasterCard: 1800 120 113

Visa: 1800 450 346

🌏 General Information

🌏 Public Holidays

1 January: New Year's Day

26 January: Australia Day

March/April: Good Friday

March/April: Easter Monday

25 April: Anzac Day

23 June: The Queen's Birthday

25 December: Christmas

26 December: Boxing Day

There are various holidays that are celebrated at state level or within certain religious communities.

🌏 Time Zones

The Australian continent is divided into three different time zones. The eastern states of Queensland, Victoria and New South Wales, as well as the Australian Capital Territory and Tasmania fall under Australian East Standard Time (AEST), which can be calculated as Greenwich Mean Time/Co-ordinated

Universal Time (GMT/UTC) +10. Australian Central Standard Time (ACST) is used in the Northern Territory, South Australia and in the town of Broken Hill, which is found in the western part of New South Wales. Australian Central Standard Time can be calculated as Greenwich Mean Time/Co-ordinated Universal Time (GMT/UTC) +9 and a half hour. Western Australia uses Australian Western Standard time, which can be calculated as Greenwich Mean Time/Co-ordinated Universal Time (GMT/UTC) +8.

Daylight Savings Time

For Daylight Savings Time, clocks are set forward by one hour at 2am on the first Sunday in October and set back one hour at 3am on the first Sunday in April. Queensland, Western Australia and the Northern Territory do not observe Daylight Savings Time.

School Holidays

In Australia, the academic year runs from January to December. Generally, schools open towards the end of January or very early in February. There is a 2 to 3 week break from the end of March or early in April, a winter vacation in June/July and a 2 week spring break in September or October. The summer vacation is usually from mid December to the end of January. Exact dates are set by the state authority in question and may vary.

Trading Hours

Trading hours are set at state rather than national level, but in most states there are little or no restrictions on hours. Generally, shopping hours in Australia are from 8am to 9pm on weekdays, 8am to 5.30pm on Saturdays and 9am to 6pm on Sundays. Most non-essential businesses will be closed on ANZAC Day, Good Friday and Christmas Day. In South Australia, trade on Sundays and Public Holidays are restricted to the hours between 11am and 5pm. In Queensland, most shopping centers close at 5pm, but will stay open for late trade on one day of the week. In Western Australia, large businesses and chain stores are restricted to trading between 9am and 5pm from Monday to Saturday and between 11am and 5pm on Sundays and Public Holidays.

🌏 Driving Policy

Australians drive on the left hand side of the road. In most states, you will be able to drive on a foreign licence, provided that it is valid and that an English translation (or International Driver's Licence) is available. The minimum driving age varies from 16 years and 6 months in the Northern Territory to 18 in Victoria, but in most states it is 17 years. The speed limit is 60km per hour for cities and urban areas, 50km per hour in suburban areas and 110km per hour on highways and rural roads. Laws regarding texting and the use of cell phones while driving vary, but in most states, a hands-free kit is required. Learner drivers or inexperienced drivers are not allowed to handle their phones at all while driving. The legal limit for drinking and driving is a Blood Alcohol Concentration (BAC) of 0.05%, but learner drivers and inexperienced drivers are not allowed to drink at all when driving.

🌏 Drinking Policy

In Australia, the minimum drinking age is 18. Children under the age of 18 are only allowed on licenced premises, if accompanied by a parent. Only businesses with a liquor licence are allowed to supply alcohol to the public and by law, they are required to ask customers and patrons for some form of identification. Local councils in Australia have the power to declare an area a dry zone, which means that no alcohol may be consumed there. The ban may relate to a particular event or can apply on an ongoing basis.

Smoking Policy

In the early 1990s, Australia introduced legislation to restrict smoking in public places. Smoking is banned in restaurants, bars and licenced clubs, although there are designated smoking areas. Recently, the ban was widened to include smoking in vehicles with children under the age of 18. Smoking is also forbidden in outdoor play areas for children, at swimming pools, bus stops and railway stations. In New South Wales, you may not smoke within 4m of a building entrance and in Western Australia, smoking is prohibited in the patrolled areas of beaches. All tobacco products are required by law to carry health warnings.

 Electricity

Electricity: 230 volts

Frequency: 50 Hz

Australia's electricity sockets are compatible with the Type I plugs, a plug that features three rectangular pins or prongs, arranged in a triangular shape, with two of the pins set at opposing angles to each other. They are similar to the plugs and sockets used in Fiji. If travelling from the USA or Canada, you will also need a power converter or transformer to convert the voltage from 230 to 110, to avoid damage to your appliances. The latest models of certain types of camcorders, cell phones and digital cameras are dual-voltage, which means that they were manufactured with a built in converter, but you will have to consult your electronics dealer about that.

Food & Drink

When they have the time for a hearty breakfast, Australians love a fry-up similar to the full English breakfast with eggs, bacon, sausage, mushroom and baked beans. Other popular breakfast options include porridge, cereal and milk or simply a slice of toast with vegemite - that is Australia's twist on good old Marmite. Technically, Australia lies in the Orient and a robust community of Asian immigrants has ensured the enduring popularity of Asian cuisine. Australia also sometimes offers exotic game, in the form of kangaroo, emu and crocodile steak. Adventurous diners will want to sample bush food, but it is not for the faint of heart. Bush tucker originated with the hunter-gatherer lifestyle of Australia's Aboriginal people and incorporates a variety of home-grown fruits and vegetables, as well as edible seeds and insects. One of the best known delicacies is the witchetty grub, which can be eaten raw or cooked. Other indigenous staples include bush yam, bush banana, conkleberries and wattle seeds.

In Australia, beer is serious business, complete with its own lingo of buzz phrases. Australians refer to a can as a "tinnie", a case of 24 cans as a "slab" and a bottle of beer as a "brownie" or, in the case of a long-necked bottle, as a "tally". While a short-necked bottle is called a "stubby", do not mistake it with a "Darwin stubby", the Northern Territory variety with a 2.25 litre capacity. Even glasses are divided into "pints", "schooners", "middys" or "pots", according to size, and you should say "My shout" to announce your intention to buy the next round.

The most popular beer brands in Australia are VB (Victoria Bitter) and Castlemaine's XXXX Gold and other beers worth sampling include Carlton Draught, Toohey's Extra Dry, Hahn Premium Light, Crown Lager, Pure Blonde and James Boag's Premium. In Queensland and New South Wales, Bundeberg beer is another favorite. Australia has a robust wine industry, of which the best known export is Penfolds Grange. Other well established wineries are Wolf Blass, Lindemans, Rosemount, Jacob's Creek, Yalumba, Berri Estates, Yellowglen and Hardy Wine Co. Tasmania produces top notch whiskies, such as the award-winning Sullivan's Cove and great cider, such as Red Sails, Lost Pippin and Pagan Cider. When it comes to soft drinks, Coca-Cola rules. Australia's taste for coffee has been influenced by the significant community of Italian immigrants. Visiting techno-geeks can try the newly launched Smartcup, an Australian invention which can be linked to a CafePay app and lets you pay for your daily brew online.

 Useful Websites

http://www.australia.com/en
http://wikitravel.org/en/Australia
https://www.australianexplorer.com/

BRISBANE, GOLD COAST & SUNSHINE COAST TRAVEL GUIDE

http://www.downundr.com/tips-and-tricks/top-ten-destinations

http://www.britz.com.au/

http://www.driveaustralia.com.au/suggested-routes/

http://ozyroadtripper.com.au/

http://australiaroadtrip.co.uk/

https://www.ozexperience.com/

Made in the USA
Lexington, KY
22 May 2017